The Spectacular Lives of Sharks

written by Annabel Griffin

illustrated by Rose Wilkinson

CONTENTS

WHAT'S SPECTACULAR ABOUT SHARKS?

Fearful foes or fantastic fish? Let's dive into the weird and wonderful world of sharks and discover what makes them so incredible.

Sizing up sharks

There are over 500 different types of shark. They come in lots of different shapes and sizes.

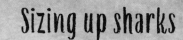

Dwarf lanternshark: The World's Smallest Shark

Whale shark: The World's Largest Shark

Great white shark

Smart hunters

Almost all sharks are **carnivores**, and many are incredible hunters with super sharp senses...and teeth!

Ninja lanternshark

Special skills

Sharks have been ruling the seas for millions of years. In that time, many have **evolved** to have some amazing features. Did you know some sharks can actually glow in the dark?

Mighty but misunderstood

A lot of them can seem pretty scary but it's very rare for sharks to attack humans. Most of them are completely harmless.

Tiger shark

SEA MONSTERS OF THE PAST

Hundreds of millions of years before dinosaurs roamed the Earth, some sharks were already swimming in the oceans!

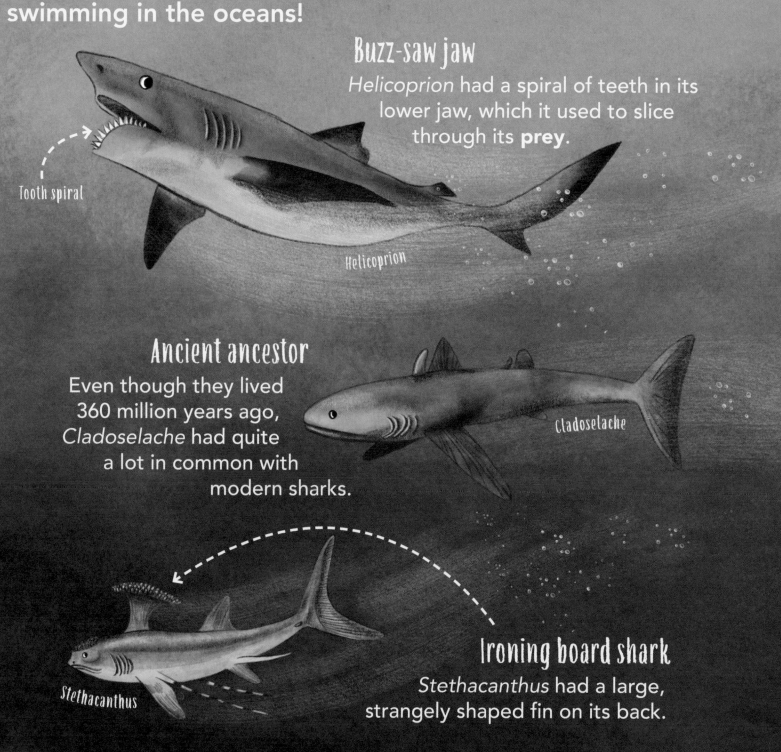

Buzz-saw jaw

Helicoprion had a spiral of teeth in its lower jaw, which it used to slice through its **prey**.

Tooth spiral

Helicoprion

Ancient ancestor

Even though they lived 360 million years ago, *Cladoselache* had quite a lot in common with modern sharks.

Cladoselache

Ironing board shark

Stethacanthus had a large, strangely shaped fin on its back.

Stethacanthus

Shark Timeline:

(mya = millions of years ago)

450 mya
Evidence exists of shark **ancestors** this far back

410 mya
Acanthodians evolve (ancient shark ancestors)

380 mya
Cladoselache evolves

Mega shark!
The biggest ever shark, the *Megalodon* was probably between 50 – 60 feet (15 – 18 m) long. Thats over three times longer than the largest *great white shark!*

Megalodon

360 mya
Stethancanthus and *Helicoprion* evolve

243 mya
The first dinosaurs start to appear

200-145 mya
The *Jurassic Period*. Most modern shark groups develop in this period

20 mya
Megalodon and first *hammerhead sharks* evolve

SHARK BODIES

Sharks are perfectly designed for swimming through water. While they come in different shapes and sizes, they all have similar features.

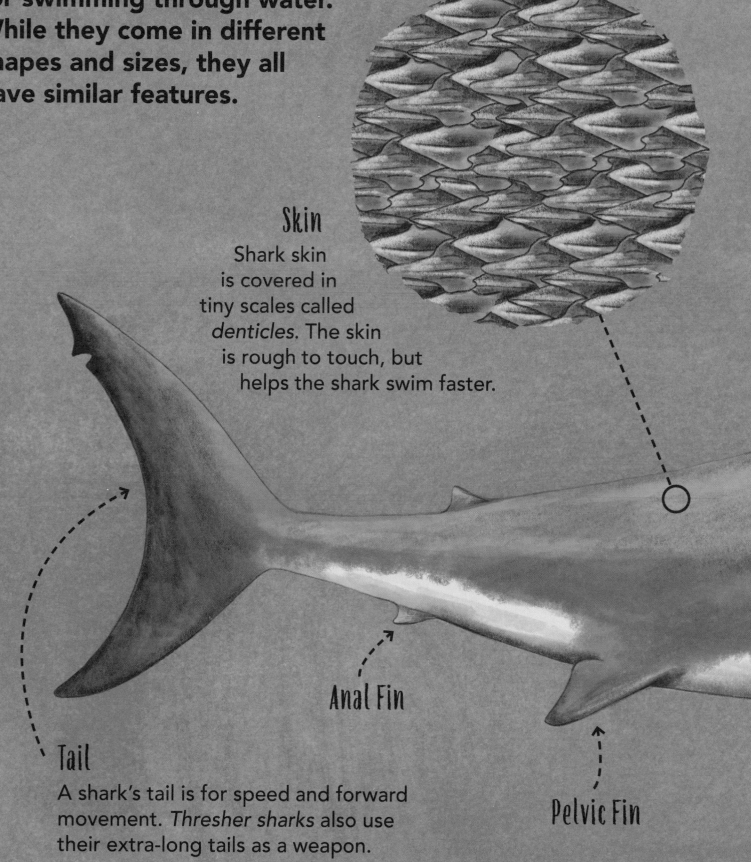

Skin

Shark skin is covered in tiny scales called *denticles*. The skin is rough to touch, but helps the shark swim faster.

Anal Fin

Pelvic Fin

Tail

A shark's tail is for speed and forward movement. *Thresher sharks* also use their extra-long tails as a weapon.

Dorsal Fin
Helps keep the shark steady.

Skeleton
Shark skeletons aren't made of bone. They are made of **cartilage**, which is much lighter and more flexible. Our noses and ears are made from the same stuff!

Gills
Gills are slits in a shark's sides, which they use to breathe.

Pectoral Fin
These fins are a bit like the wings on a plane. They are used for balance and steering.

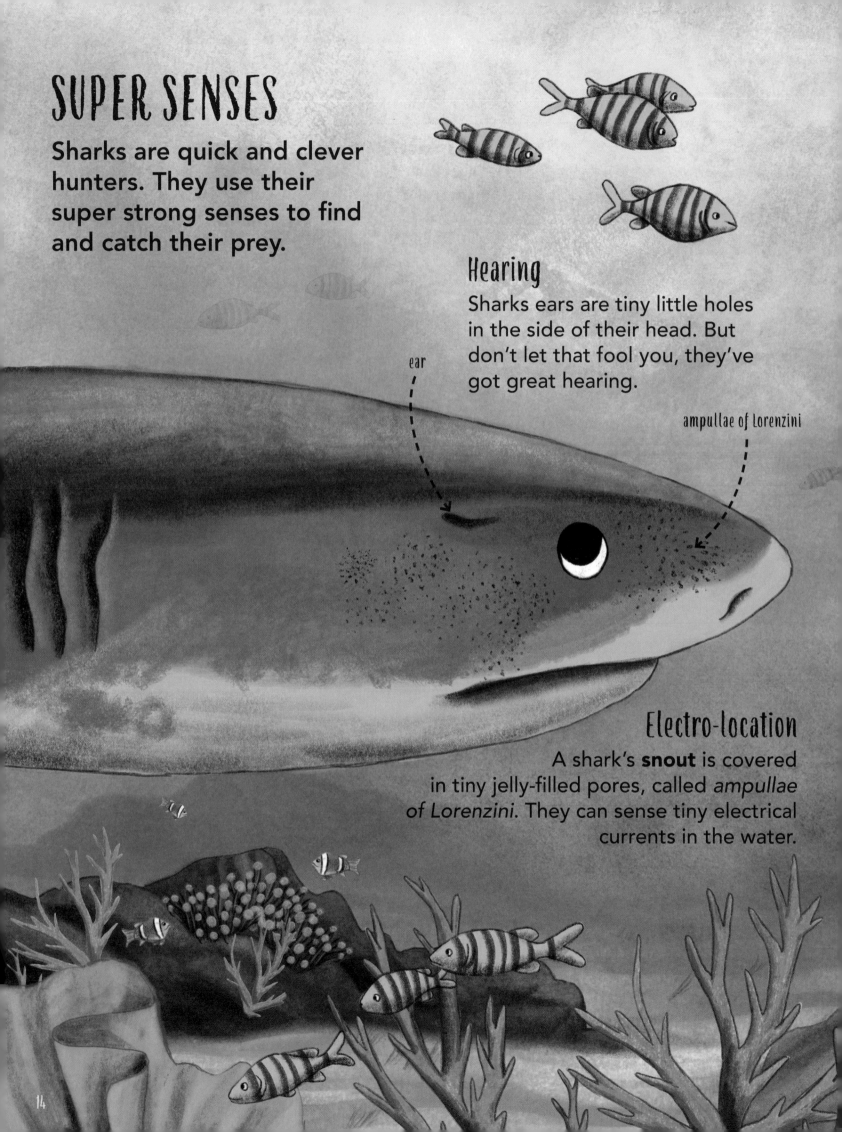

SUPER SENSES

Sharks are quick and clever hunters. They use their super strong senses to find and catch their prey.

Hearing

Sharks ears are tiny little holes in the side of their head. But don't let that fool you, they've got great hearing.

ear

ampullae of Lorenzini

Electro-location

A shark's **snout** is covered in tiny jelly-filled pores, called *ampullae of Lorenzini*. They can sense tiny electrical currents in the water.

Smell
A shark could smell just one drop of blood mixed with one million drops of water!

Sight
Having eyes far apart on the side of their heads means that sharks can see in almost all directions.

Tiger shark

Lunch bell?
Some sharks have barbels hanging down from their snouts. These help them find prey.

Blind shark

barbel

TEETH AND JAWS

A shark's teeth are its greatest weapon, so it's important for them to have a nice sharp set at all times.

Out with the old...

Some sharks lose 30,000 teeth in their lifetime! They replace them regularly as they are easily damaged.

...In with the new

They have many rows of teeth and make new ones all the time. When a tooth falls out, the one behind moves forward to take its place.

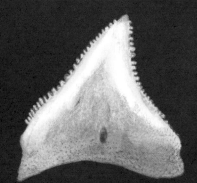

Tiger shark tooth

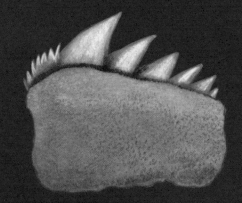

Sevengill cow shark tooth

Bull shark tooth

Jutting Jaws

Some sharks, like the *great white*, have jaws that aren't firmly attached to their skull. This means they can push them forward to take big, powerful bites.

Some shark teeth have **serrated** edges to tear through flesh.

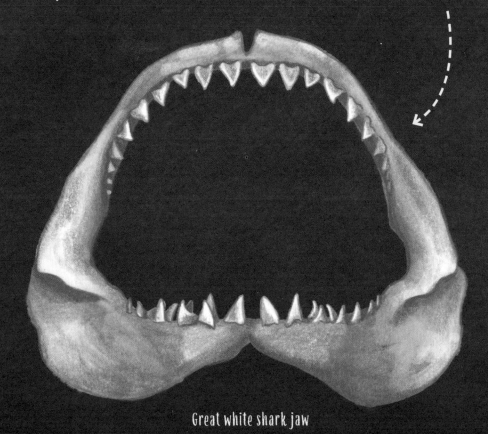

Great white shark jaw

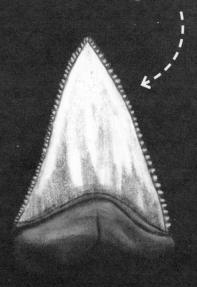

Great white shark tooth

Long, thin teeth are good for piercing and holding onto prey.

Whale sharks have around 3,000 tiny teeth, but they don't actually use them!

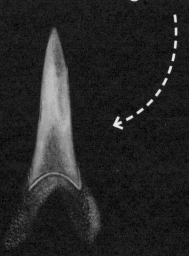

Sand tiger shark tooth

Goblin shark tooth

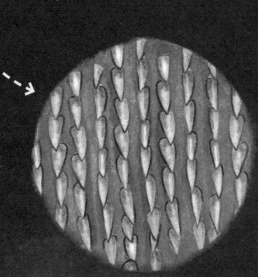

A section of whale shark teeth

BABY SHARKS

Baby sharks are called pups. Some sharks give birth to live pups, while others lay eggs.

Shark nurseries

Some sharks lay eggs, or give birth, in safe waters, known as *nurseries*. Nurseries offer pups protection until they are old enough to defend themselves.

Lemon shark pup - - >

A catshark **fetus** inside its eggcase.

A *yolk sac* provides nutrients to help the shark grow.

Tendrils grip onto things to stop the eggcase floating away.

Mangrove tree roots

Underwater treehouse

Mangrove forests, like this one, make good nurseries. The tree roots are the perfect pup hideout. No big predators allowed!

Mermaids' Purses

An empty eggcase is known as a *mermaid's purse.* You can tell what kind of shark hatched, based on the shape.

Large spotted catshark

Ghost shark (chimaera)

Australian swellshark

Horn shark

GLOW IN THE DARK SHARKS

**Some sharks have an amazing superpower...
they can glow in the dark!**

Why glow?

There are different reasons why sharks might glow. It could attract prey, scare off predators, be used as **camouflage**, or for communicating with other sharks.

Kitefin shark

Big and bright

The kitefin shark is the largest-known **luminous** fish. It can grow to as large as 5.9 feet (180 cm) long.

Ninja lanternshark

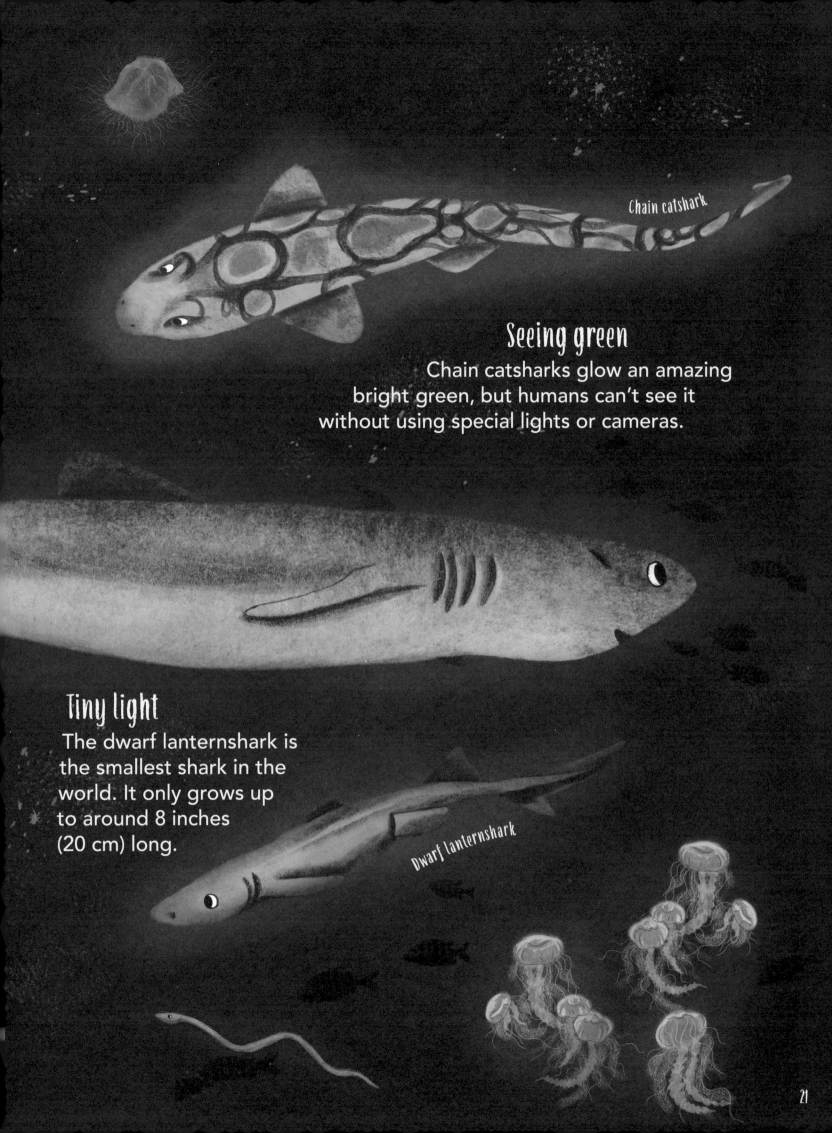

Chain catshark

Seeing green

Chain catsharks glow an amazing bright green, but humans can't see it without using special lights or cameras.

Tiny light

The dwarf lanternshark is the smallest shark in the world. It only grows up to around 8 inches (20 cm) long.

Dwarf lanternshark

GREAT WHITE SHARK

When you think of a shark, it's probably the image of a great white that comes to mind.

A great size

Great whites are the largest **predatory** fish on Earth. They can grow to around 20 feet (6 m) long.

Hungry hunters

A great white's diet includes other sharks, fish, shellfish, sea birds, seals, sea lions, and even some whales.

Big splash

They sometimes jump right out of the water when chasing their prey.

Humans not on the menu

On the very rare occasion that a great white bites a human, it usually spits them back out. They probably don't think we taste very nice!

BASKING SHARK

These sharks might look scary, with their big gaping mouths, but they are actually completely harmless.

Second prize

The basking shark is the world's second largest fish. They are usually around 26 feet (8 m) long.

Big mouth, tiny food

They mostly eat tiny sea creatures called *zooplankton*, but sometimes catch small fish too.

Lazy diners

Basking sharks don't hunt for food. They just swim around with their mouths wide open and wait for dinner to swim in.

Down the hatch

Their style of eating is called *filter feeding*. Their large gills are specially designed to let water out, while trapping any food.

gills

GOBLIN SHARK

These rare sharks have got to be one of the creepiest creatures in the sea!

Ancient history

Known as "living fossils", they are the only living members of an ancient family of sharks dating back 125 million years!

Nosey!

The goblin shark's most remarkable feature is its long, pointy snout.

Monster of the deep

Goblin sharks aren't often seen by humans. They live in the deep sea, 330 to 4,260 feet (100-1,300 m) below the surface.

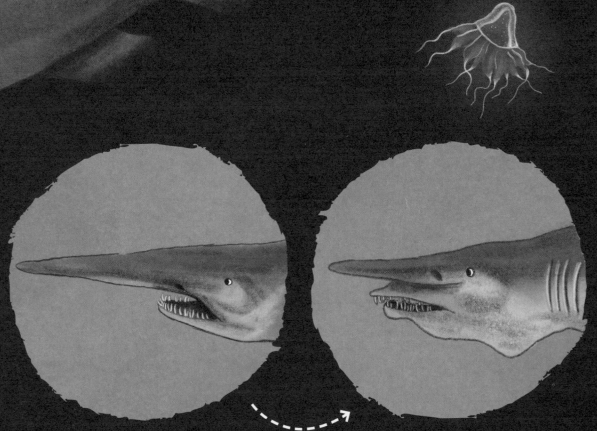

Snappy Jaws

They can extend their jaws forward at lightning speed to grab their prey. This makes them look even weirder!

GREAT HAMMERHEAD SHARK

There are nine different types of hammerhead shark. They all have extra wide heads. The *great hammerhead* is the biggest of them all.

Stinging snack

Hammerheads love to eat stingrays. They use their big heads to pin them to the ocean floor.

Why the wide face?

The wide shape of their head allows them to see all around them at once.

Lone rangers

They are big loners and will travel long distances on their own.

Low swimmers

They spend a lot of time swimming along the bottom of the ocean, looking for food.

WHALE SHARK

Introducing the world's biggest fish! The largest known whale shark was over 59 feet (18 m) long. That's almost as long as a bowling lane!

Gentle giants

Whale sharks are harmless to humans. They are filter feeders, and only eat plankton, krill and small fish.

One of a kind

Every whale shark's spots and stripes are completely **unique**.

A big mouthful

They may look toothless from a distance, but their mouths are filled with over 300 rows of tiny teeth.

Open wide

Their mouths can measure up to 5 ft (1.5m) wide. That's big enough to fit round a double bed!

GREENLAND SHARK

These large sharks are found in the freezing waters of the Arctic Ocean and the North Atlantic.

Old timers

Greenland sharks have one of the longest **lifespans** of any creature on Earth. Some scientists think that some of them have lived to be over 400 years old!

Frozen fish

Their flesh contains special chemicals that stop their bodies from freezing in the cold water. They also make them poisonous to eat.

Bad company

Most Greenland sharks have **parasites** hanging from their eyes. These tiny sea creatures make them go blind. Luckily the sharks can use their other senses to get around.

Slow and steady

They swim very slowly to save energy in the cold. They usually travel at under one mile per hour!

WOBBEGONG

These funny looking sharks are masters of disguise. They spend most of their time on the seabed, pretending to be rocks or coral.

The element of surprise

Instead of going hunting, wobbegong will lie in wait for unsuspecting prey to swim past. Then they pounce!

Funny face

No good disguise is complete without a fake beard! These frilly bits, called *dermal lobes*, also help to attract prey.

Cunning camouflage

There are 12 different types of wobbegong. They all have different patterns that are designed to make them difficult to spot.

Laying low

Their wide, flat body shape makes it easy to blend in with the seabed.

view from above

SAWSHARK

Sawsharks get their name
from their unusual snouts,
which look like chainsaws.

Special weapon

Their snouts are lined with teeth
around the edge. They use
them to slash at their prey.

Little saw

Sawsharks are quite small.
The largest they will grow to
is 5 feet (152 cm) in length.

mouth

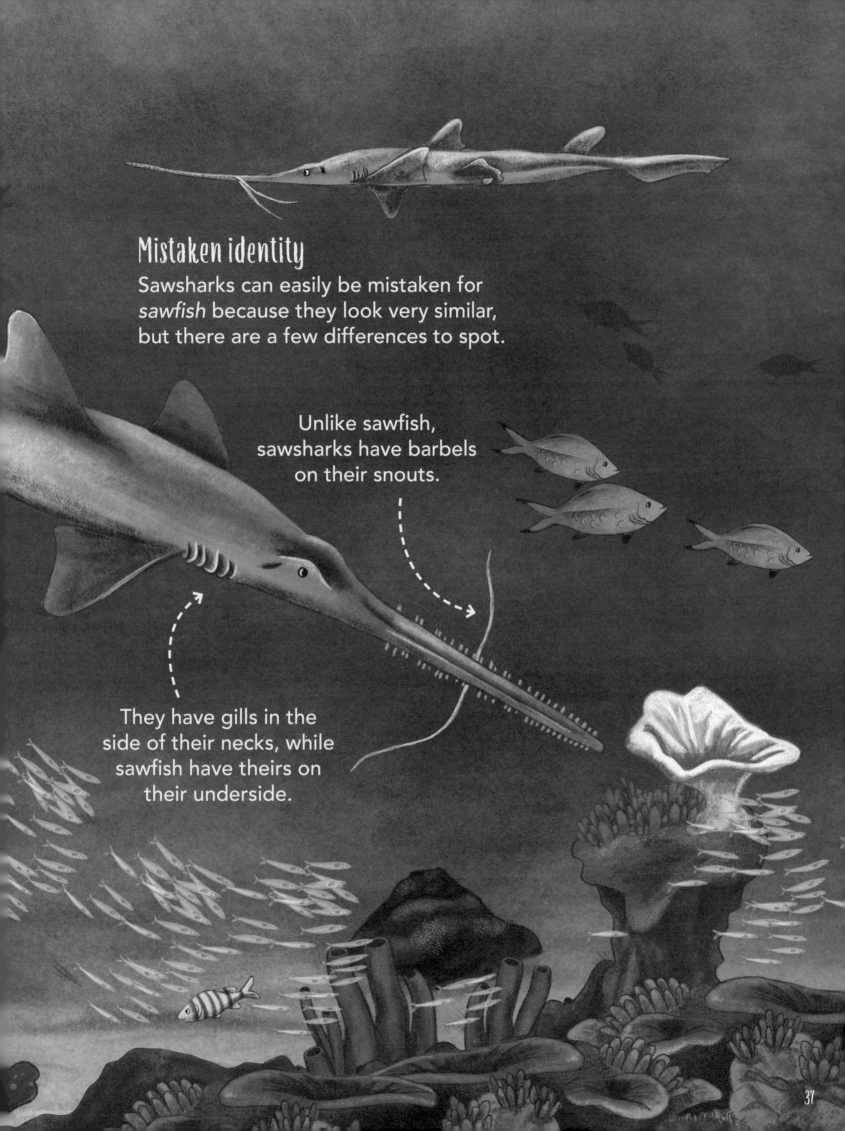

Mistaken identity

Sawsharks can easily be mistaken for *sawfish* because they look very similar, but there are a few differences to spot.

Unlike sawfish, sawsharks have barbels on their snouts.

They have gills in the side of their necks, while sawfish have theirs on their underside.

HORN SHARK

These slow-moving sharks get their name from the spines on their backs, which look a bit like horns.

Don't touch me!
Their horn-like spines are poisonous and used to protect them from predators.

purple sea urchin

Not a strong swimmer
They stay close to the seabed and use their lower fins to crawl along the rocks.

Crunchy snacks
They like to eat hard shellfish.
Eating lots of purple sea urchins
can turn their teeth purple!

See you, sucker!
They use their pig-like snout
to suck food into their mouth.
They have special flat teeth at
the back of their mouth for
crunching down on shellfish.

FRILLED SHARK

With its long, eel-like body and terrifying teeth, this deep-sea creature looks more like a sea serpent than a shark!

Squid dinner

Most of their diet is made up of different types of squid.

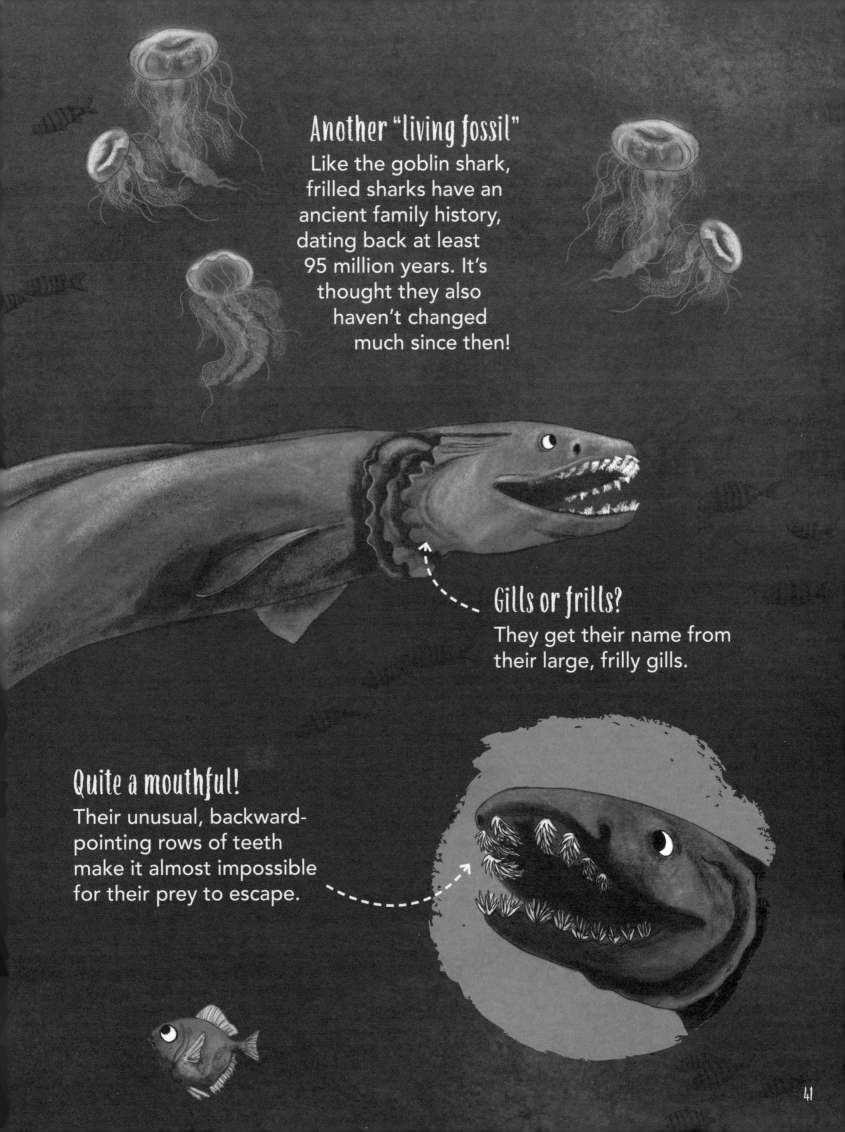

Another "living fossil"

Like the goblin shark, frilled sharks have an ancient family history, dating back at least 95 million years. It's thought they also haven't changed much since then!

Gills or frills?

They get their name from their large, frilly gills.

Quite a mouthful!

Their unusual, backward-pointing rows of teeth make it almost impossible for their prey to escape.

COOKIECUTTER SHARK

Watch out! They may be less that 2 feet (60 cm) long, but these freaky looking sharks have a pretty big bite!

Big bite

When it opens its mouth wide, its jaw makes the shape of a circular cookie cutter. Perfect for taking cookie-sized bites!

This sucks!

They use their big lips to suck onto prey, like a plunger. Then, they sink their teeth in and spin around, to cut out a chunk.

Pick on someone your own size!

These sharks go after much larger animals, including dolphins, whales, and other sharks. They're even brave enough to bite a *great white*!

Just a nibble

Cookiecutter sharks leave their victims alive, but with a few chunks missing!

SCARED OF SHARKS?

Sharks have a reputation for being big, scary man-eaters. In reality, most sharks are completely harmless to humans.

Look out for signs

On some beaches where shark sightings are common, signs are posted to tell you if it's safe to enter the water.

What are the chances?

Shark attacks are extremely rare. You have a much higher chance of being killed by a firework than by a shark, and that's very, very unlikely!

Surfers not seals

Surfers are the most likely to be attacked because sharks might mistake a surfboard for a seal. This is still incredibly rare.

Mistaken identity

Sharks don't really want to eat people. It is thought that most shark attacks happen because the shark has mistaken the person for something else. They will often take one bite and then let go.

WHY SHARKS MATTER

We often focus on sharks as ferocious killers, but many other sea creatures rely on them for survival.

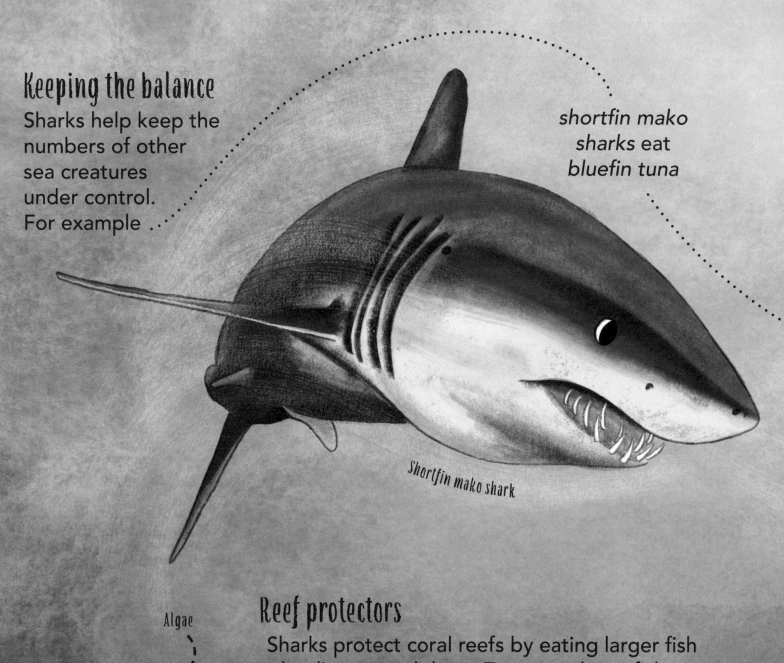

Keeping the balance

Sharks help keep the numbers of other sea creatures under control. For example ...

shortfin mako sharks eat bluefin tuna

Shortfin mako shark

Algae

Reef protectors

Sharks protect coral reefs by eating larger fish that live around them. Too many large fish would mean that lots of smaller ones would get eaten. Without small fish to eat **algae**, reefs can become smothered in it, making them unhealthy.

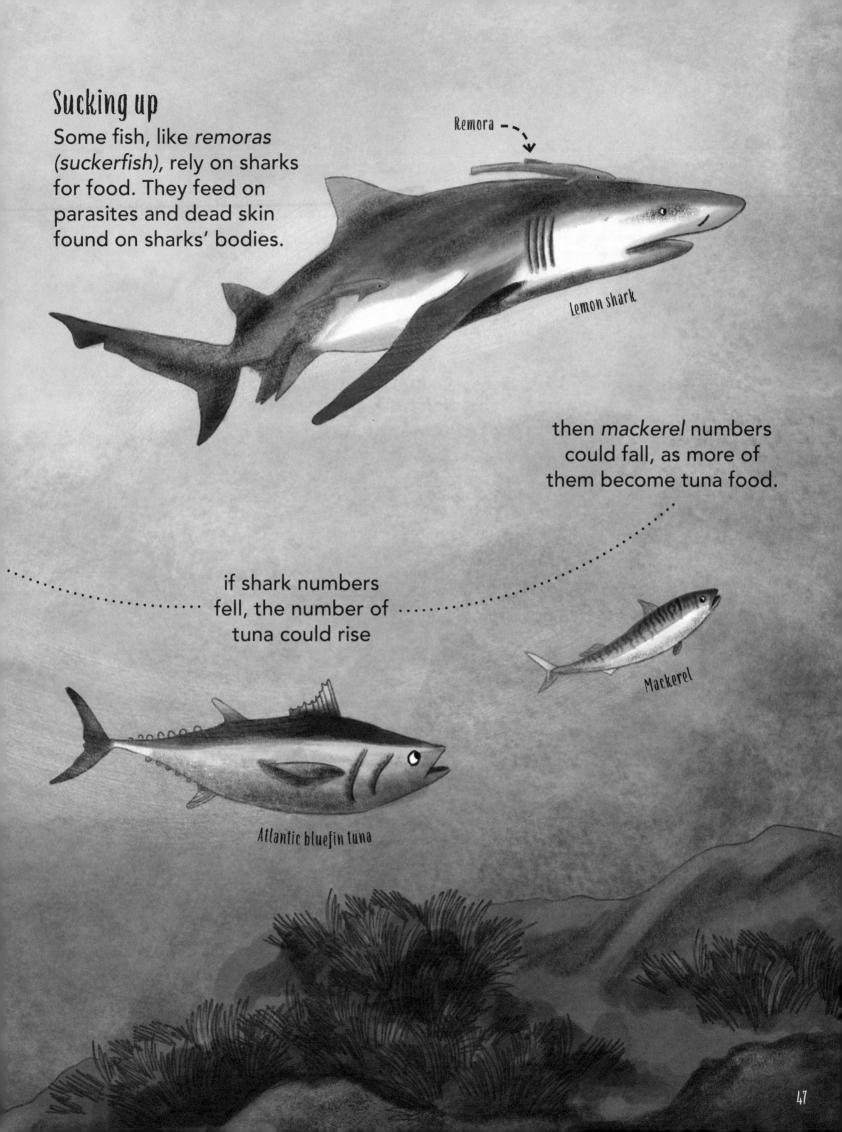

Sucking up

Some fish, like *remoras* (*suckerfish*), rely on sharks for food. They feed on parasites and dead skin found on sharks' bodies.

Remora

Lemon shark

then *mackerel* numbers could fall, as more of them become tuna food.

if shark numbers fell, the number of tuna could rise

Mackerel

Atlantic bluefin tuna

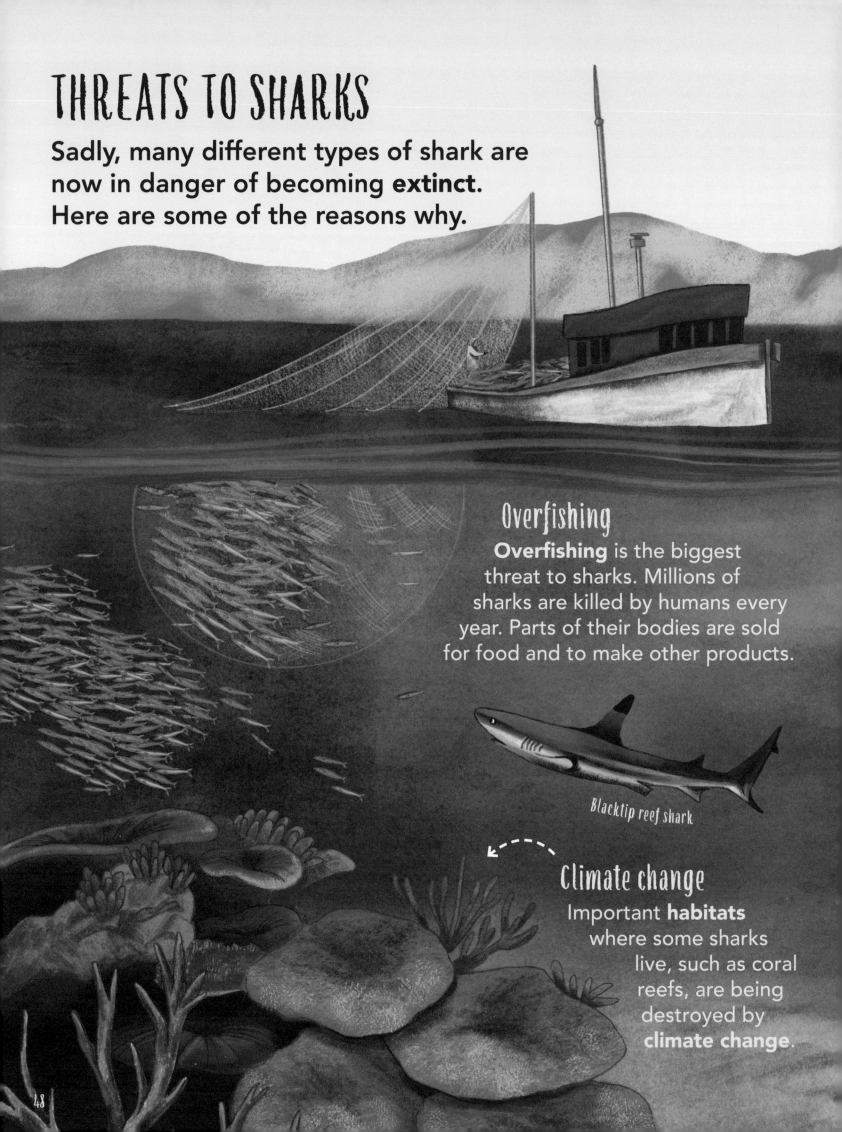

THREATS TO SHARKS

Sadly, many different types of shark are now in danger of becoming **extinct**. Here are some of the reasons why.

Overfishing

Overfishing is the biggest threat to sharks. Millions of sharks are killed by humans every year. Parts of their bodies are sold for food and to make other products.

Blacktip reef shark

Climate change

Important **habitats** where some sharks live, such as coral reefs, are being destroyed by **climate change**.

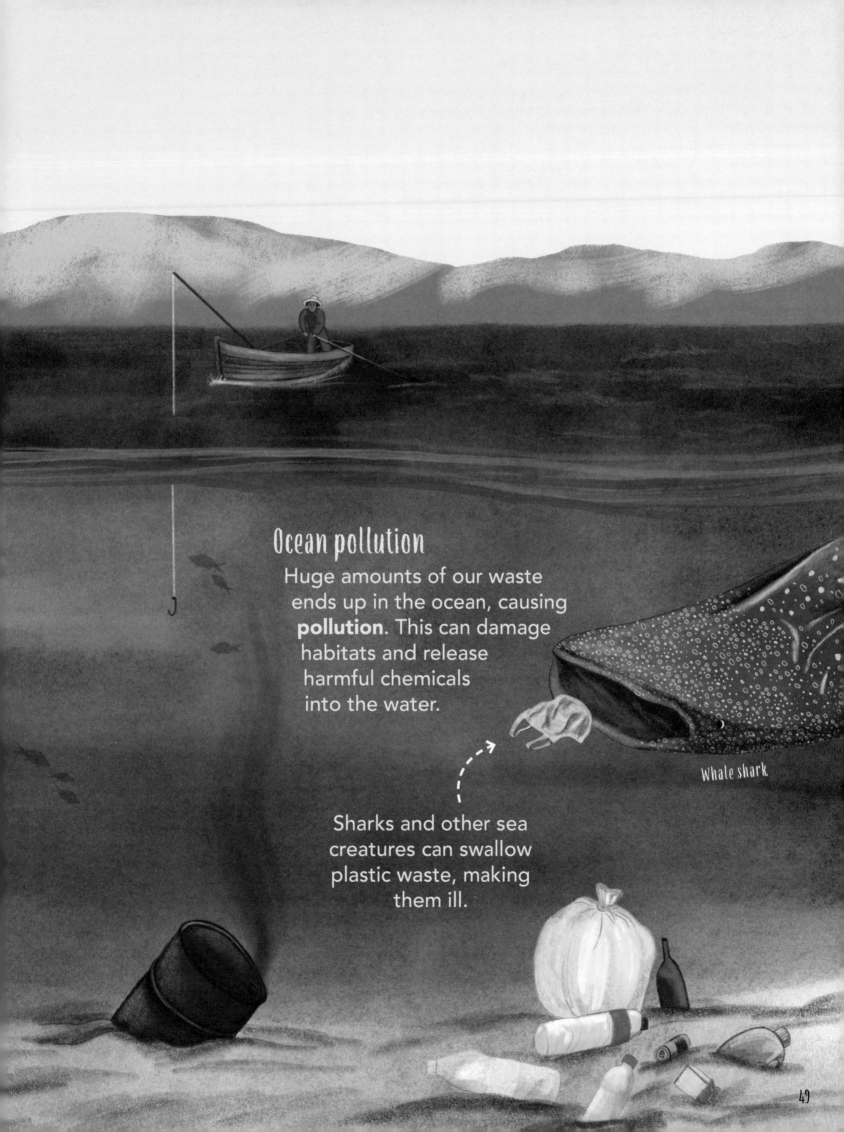

Ocean pollution

Huge amounts of our waste ends up in the ocean, causing **pollution**. This can damage habitats and release harmful chemicals into the water.

Whale shark

Sharks and other sea creatures can swallow plastic waste, making them ill.

ENDANGERED SHARKS

Many sharks are now **critically endangered**. This means there is a high risk of them becoming extinct if nothing is done to save them. Here are some of the most endangered species.

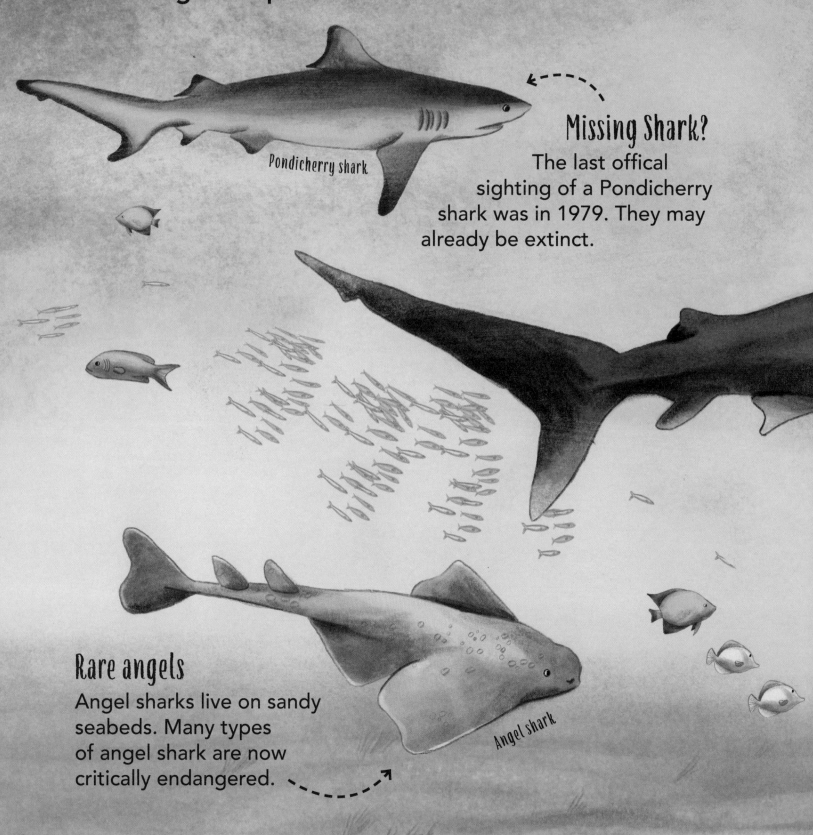

Pondicherry shark

Missing Shark?

The last offical sighting of a Pondicherry shark was in 1979. They may already be extinct.

Rare angels

Angel sharks live on sandy seabeds. Many types of angel shark are now critically endangered.

Angel shark

Famous but fragile
Hammerhead sharks are probably one of the best known shark families, but some of its members are in serious danger.

Scalloped hammerhead

Oceaninc whitetip shark

Big fins, big problems!
Oceanic whitetips are overfished for their large fins, which are used to make *shark fin soup*, a popular dish in parts of Southeast Asia.

Daggernose shark

Wrong place, wrong time
These rare sharks are in danger from being caught accidentally in fishing nets.

SWIMMING WITH SHARKS

Shark tourism can make many people's dreams of diving with sharks come true. Would you be brave enough?

Hammerhead shark

Helping sharks

Shark tourism can be good for sharks as local people can make their money from tourists rather than fishing for sharks.

Tiger shark

Shark watch

Many **tourists** prefer watching sharks from the safety of a boat, but boats that get too close can harm the sharks.

Cage diving

Cage diving can be a good way to see more dangerous sharks up close, as the steel cage protects the divers.

Great white shark

Should you feed sharks?

Some diving tours allow you to feed sharks, but some people believe this could lead to more shark attacks, as sharks might start to think people equal food.

SAVING SHARKS

With so many endangered sharks, what is being done to protect them, and how can we help?

Keeping track

Scientists attach **tracking devices** (or tags) to shark's fins. This allows them to track their movement and habits, and keep an eye on their numbers.

SCIENCE SAVES SHARKS

CLEAN UP OUR

Stop overfishing

Shark sanctuaries are areas of ocean where shark fishing is forbidden. Many countries have now set up sanctuaries in areas that they control.

Did you know?

Shark meat is sold as food in some countries.

Fins are the main ingredient in shark fin soup.

Shark skin is turned into a type of leather.

Shark liver oil is used in many beauty products and some medicines.

SHOP SMART

Avoid food and other products that contain shark parts.

SHARKS ARE FRIENDS, NOT FOOD!

OCEANS

Many people around the world are working hard to clean up plastics and pollution in our oceans. You can help by **recycling** and not buying plastic products.

WHO DIVES DEEPEST?

Some sharks have been known to dive to incredible depths in the ocean.

Sea level

Sunlight zone

656 ft (200 m)

Twilight zone

Blacktip reef shark
Dive range: 0 – 300 ft (0 – 92 m)

Lemon shark
Dive range: 0 – 300 ft (0 – 92 m)

Daggernose shark
Dive range: 13 – 130 ft (4 – 40 m)

Great hammerhead shark
Dive range: 0 – 985 ft (0 – 300 m)

Common sawshark
Dive range: 130 – 2060 ft (40 – 630 m)

Although some sharks can dive very deep, most of them spend almost all their time in the sunlight zone.

This chart shows sharks at around the deepest depths that they have been found.

56

3,280 ft
(1,000 m)

Oceanic whitetip shark
Dive range: 0 – 3,550 ft (0 – 1,080 m)

Great white shark
Dive range: 0 – 3,940 ft (0 – 1,200 m)

Goblin shark
Dive range: 0 – 4,260 ft (0 – 1,300 m)

Frilled shark
Dive range: 160 – 4,920 ft (50 – 1,500 m)

The deeper you dive, the darker it gets. The ocean is split into zones according to the amount of sunlight there is. There is complete darkness in the midnight zone.

Basking shark
Dive range: 0 – 4,140 ft (0 – 1,260 m)

Greenland shark
Dive range: 0 – 8,680 ft (0 – 2,650 m)

Whale shark
Dive range: 0 – 6,320 ft (0 – 1,930 m)

Cookiecutter shark
Dive range: 0 – 11,480 ft (0 – 3,500 m)

Midnight zone

GLOSSARY

algae
Plant-like living things that usually live in or near water.

ancestors
Members of a family from long ago. For instance, your great great grandmother would be an ancestor of yours.

camouflage
To look like your surroundings, to help you stay hidden.

carnivores
An animal that mostly eats meat.

cartilage
A flexible material that makes up part of many animal's bodies, including humans. Shark skeletons are made of it.

climate change
Rising temperatures on the Earth, which are affecting weather around the world. Ocean temperatures are rising too, which is causing problems for some plants and animals that live in them, including sharks.

critically endangered
At a very high risk of becoming extinct (see opposite).

evolved
Having changed or developed slowly over a long period of time.

extinct
When a type of plant or animal no longer exists anywhere on Earth.

fetus
An unborn or unhatched baby animal.

gills
A body part that sharks, and other fish, use to breathe underwater.

habitats
The place where an animal or plant lives.

lifespans
The length of time that someone or something is alive for.

luminous
Something that shines light or glows.

overfishing

When too many fish are being caught.

parasites

Living things that live on or inside another living thing to survive.

pollution

When air, water or land on Earth becomes unhealthy because of trash, chemicals, or other harmful things within it.

predatory

Hunting and killing other animals for food. Animals that do this are called predators.

prey

An animal that is hunted and killed by other animals for food.

recycling

Turning something that would otherwise be thrown away into something that can be used again.

serrated

Sharp, zig-zagged points along the edge of something, like a saw.

shark sanctuaries

An area of ocean where shark fishing has been made illegal.

shark tourism

When people pay to go and watch or dive with sharks.

snout

A long nose that sticks out from the rest of the head.

tourists

People who are on vacation.

tracking devices

Machines that attach to something so that its location can be tracked.

unique

Being the only one of its kind.

INDEX

About the Author

Annabel is a writer and artist based in Cornwall, UK, who writes children's books with a focus on animals and the natural world. She is the author of the *One Planet* series, about Earth and the environment, and *What Can I See in the Wild?*, published by Beetle Books. In her free time, Annabel enjoys drawing, hiking, and gardening. She is never without a good book.

About the Illustrator

Rose is an illustrator, artist and educator from Hereford, UK, now living and working in London. Her mediums of choice are watercolor, gouache, pencil and Procreate.

First published in 2022 by
Hungry Tomato Ltd
F1, Old Bakery Studios,
Blewetts Wharf, Malpas Road,
Truro, Cornwall, TR1 1QH, UK

Thanks to our creative team
Senior Editor: Anna Hussey
Graphic Designer: Amy Harvey
Editorial Assistant: Charlotte Moyle

A CIP catalog record for this book is available from the British Library.

Beetle Books is an imprint of Hungry Tomato.

ISBN 978-1-914087-47-9

Printed and bound in China

Discover more at:
www.mybeetlebooks.com
www.hungrytomato.com

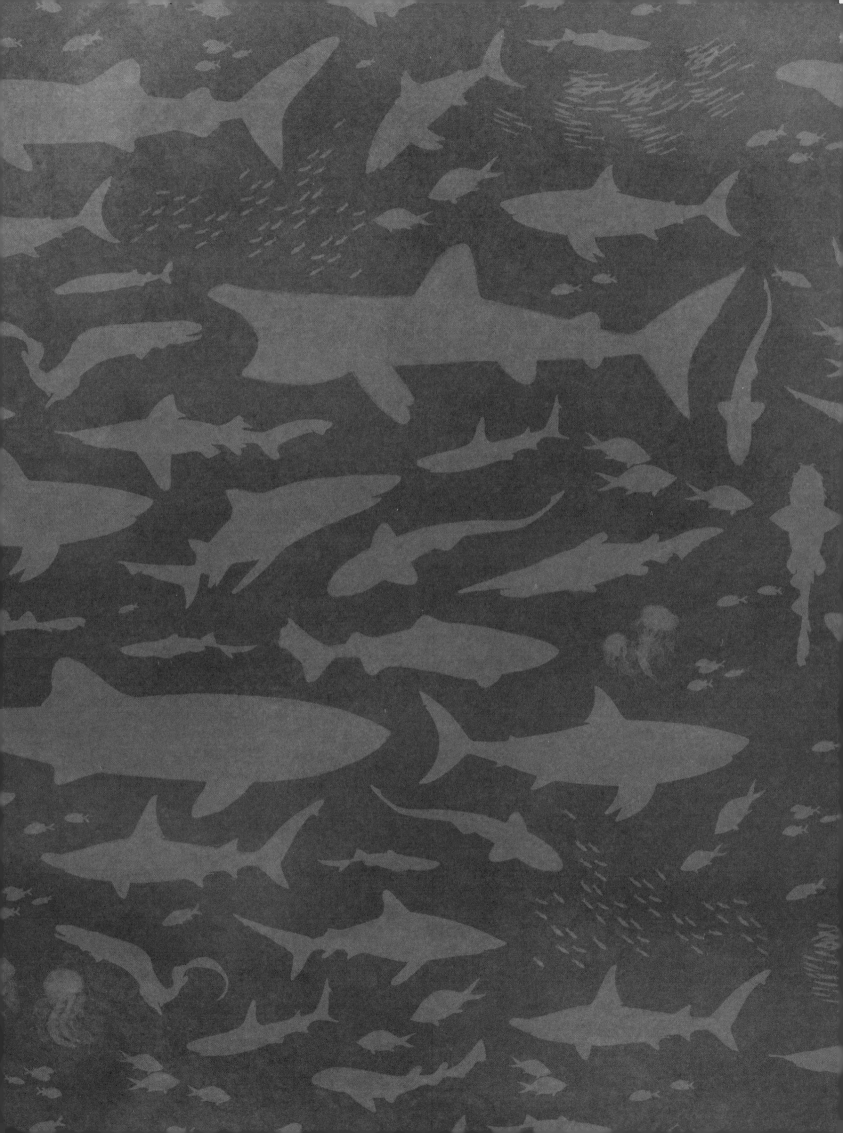